LIFE PICTURE PUZZLE

WELCOME TO LIFE'S FIFTH
PICTURE
PUZZLE
BOOK

Vacation, time off, R&R—regardless of the word we use to describe it, Americans love to get away from it all. We work hard, and we play even harder. We need breaks to keep us going. After four very successful Picture Puzzle books, LIFE decided to take a break as well. But not from creating puzzles—we're having too much fun to give that up. Instead, we thought we would approach our fifth book a little differently by picking a dedicated theme. So we began searching all over the world for images of people on vacation. Our photo editors looked for the most interesting pictures they could find of people camping, skiing, hiking, sightseeing, river rafting, or just relaxing and spending time with their families. Then we set about turning the best of these photos into our famous puzzles. What you hold in your hands is the result: our Vacation Picture Puzzle book.

Don't worry—our Vacation book has everything you know and love from our earlier efforts. There are still four levels of difficulty: novice, master, expert, and genius. For our first-time readers, we continue to start at a nice and easy pace, and for those experienced puzzlers out there, we end on a perplexing yet satisfying note. No matter your skill level, you'll find a puzzle here to challenge you. Once again, we dipped into LIFE's world-famous photo archive to create some great black-and-white puzzles for our classics section. We've worked hard on this book, and we're very proud of the result. We're sure that it is going to provide you hours of enjoyment.

If you're hungry for a whole new mind-bending adventure, rest assured that the sixth and seventh LIFE Picture Puzzle books are already on the drawing board. Our next book will focus on animals of all stripes: furry, finny, feathery, and scaly. We'll feature photos of working animals, wild animals, famous animals, and, of course, beloved household pets. When you need to satisfy an immediate, undeniable Picture Puzzle craving, check out our online archive of puzzles at *www.LIFE.com*. And don't forget to let us know what you think by dropping us a line at picturepuzzle@life.com. We'd love to hear from you.

[OUR CUT-UP PUZZLES: EASY AS 1-2-3]

We snipped a photo into four or six pieces. Then we rearranged the pieces and numbered them.

Your mission: Beneath each cut-up puzzle, write the number of the piece in the box where it belongs.

Check the answer key at the back of the book to see what the reassembled image looks like.

[HOW TO PLAY THE PUZZLES]

A Day to Remember

Get right to the heart of this puzzle

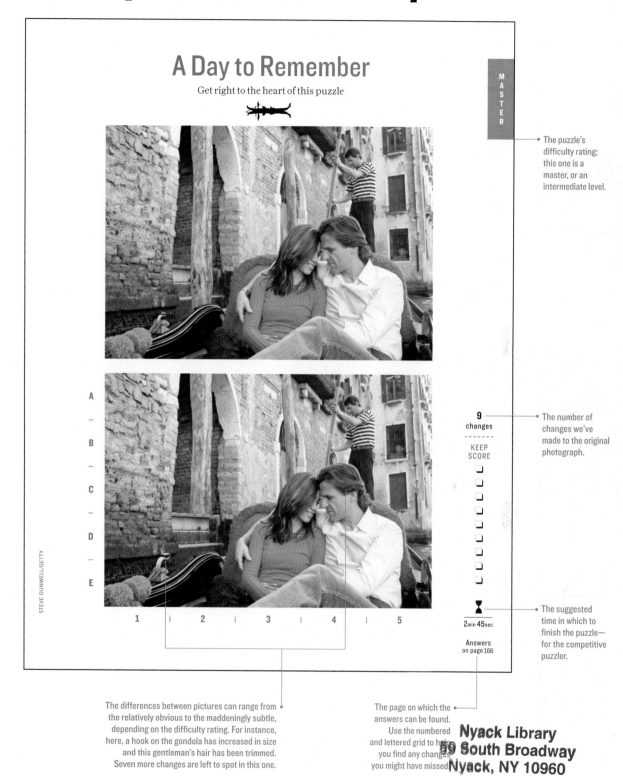

MASTER

• The puzzle's difficulty rating; this one is a master, or an intermediate level.

9 changes

• The number of changes we've made to the original photograph.

KEEP SCORE

2min 45sec

• The suggested time in which to finish the puzzle—for the competitive puzzler.

Answers on page 166

The differences between pictures can range from the relatively obvious to the maddeningly subtle, depending on the difficulty rating. For instance, here, a hook on the gondola has increased in size and this gentleman's hair has been trimmed. Seven more changes are left to spot in this one.

The page on which the answers can be found. Use the numbered and lettered grid to help you find any changes you might have missed.

LIFE PICTURE PUZZLE

Puzzle Master Michael Roseman
Editor Robert Sullivan
Deputy Editor Danielle Dowling
Director of Photography Barbara Baker Burrows
Deputy Picture Editor Christina Lieberman
Research Editor Danny Freedman
Copy Barbara Gogan, Parlan McGaw

LIFE Puzzle Books
Managing Editor Bill Shapiro
Creative Director Richard Baker

LIFE Books
President Andrew Blau
Business Manager Roger Adler
Business Development Manager Jeff Burak

Editorial Operations
Richard K. Prue, David Sloan (Directors), Richard Shaffer (Group Manager),
Brian Fellows, Raphael Joa, Angel Mass, Stanley E. Moyse, Albert Rufino (Managers),
Soheila Asayesh, Keith Aurelio, Trang Ba Chuong, Charlotte Coco, Osmar Escalona,
Kevin Hart, Norma Jones, Mert Kerimoglu, Rosalie Khan, Marco Lau, Po Fung Ng,
Rudi Papiri, Barry Pribula, Carina A. Rosario, Albert Rufino, Christopher Scala,
Diana Suryakusuma, Vaune Trachtman, Paul Tupay, Lionel Vargas, David Weiner

Time Inc. Home Entertainment
Publisher Richard Fraiman
General Manager Steven Sandonato
Executive Director, Marketing Services Carol Pittard
Director, Retail & Special Sales Tom Mifsud
Director, New Product Development Peter Harper
Assistant Director, Brand Marketing Laura Adam
Associate Counsel Helen Wan
Book Production Manager Suzanne Janso
Design & Prepress Manager Anne-Michelle Gallero
Senior Marketing Manager Joy Butts
Associate Brand Manager Shelley Rescober

Special thanks to Bozena Bannett, Alexandra Bliss, Glenn Buonocore, Susan Chodakiewicz,
Robert Marasco, Brooke Reger, Mary Sarro-Waite, Ilene Schreider, Adriana Tierno,
Alex Voznesenskiy

PUBLISHED BY

LIFE Books

Vol. 8, No. 3 • April 14, 2008

Copyright 2008
Time Inc.
1271 Avenue of the Americas
New York, New York 10020

We welcome your comments and suggestions about LIFE Books. Please write to us at:
LIFE Books
Attention: Book Editors
PO Box 11016
Des Moines, IA 50336-1016

If you would like to order any of our hardcover Collector's Edition books, please call us at 1-800-327-6388
(Monday through Friday, 7 a.m. to 8 p.m., or Saturday, 7 a.m. to 6 p.m. Central Time).

READY, SET, GO!

NOVIC

READY, SET

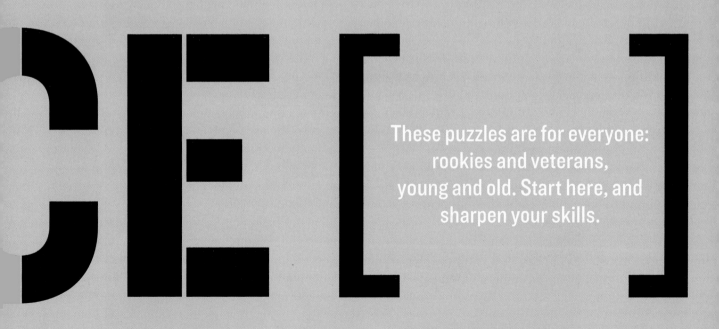

These puzzles are for everyone: rookies and veterans, young and old. Start here, and sharpen your skills.

Virtual Vacation

Take a break on the rug so you won't get sand in your sandals

A

B

C

D

E

1   2   3   4   5

11
changes

KEEP
SCORE

❏
❏
❏
❏
❏
❏
❏
❏
❏
❏
❏

⧗

2min **15**sec

Answers
on page 166

London Calling

Don't bewilder the Beefeater, or you could lose your head

11
changes

⧗

2min 20sec

Answers
on page 166

KEEP SCORE ★ ❑ ❑ ❑ ❑ ❑ ❑ ❑ ❑ ❑ ❑ ❑ ❑

Hello Mudduh, Hello Fadduh

While these kids await their summer of fun, count the ways they've changed

A

B

C

D

E

1   2   3   4   5

14
changes
- - - - - - - - -
KEEP
SCORE

❏
❏
❏
❏
❏
❏
❏
❏
❏
❏
❏
❏
❏
❏

⏳

2min 30sec

Answers
on page 166

It's All Downhill From Here

This clan is ready to ride

A
—
B
—
C
—
D
—
E

1 | 2 | 3 | 4 | 5

9
changes

⧖
3min 10sec

Answers
on page 166

KEEP SCORE ★ ❏ ❏ ❏ ❏ ❏ ❏ ❏ ❏ ❏

A Vexing Veldt

Don't worry—our hunt is cruelty-free

A
—
B
—
C
—
D
—
E

1   2   3   4   5

9
changes

⧗
3min 20sec

Answers
on page 166

KEEP SCORE ★ ❏ ❏ ❏ ❏ ❏ ❏ ❏ ❏ ❏

Everything's in the Trunk

Elephants never forget, but can you
remember how to solve this puzzle?

A
–
B
–
C
–
D
–
E

1 | 2 | 3 | 4 | 5

10
changes

⧗

3min 50sec

Answers
on page 166

KEEP SCORE ★ ❑ ❑ ❑ ❑ ❑ ❑ ❑ ❑ ❑ ❑

Put the Lime in the Coconut

In this tropical paradise, a few things have gone amiss

10
changes

KEEP
SCORE

☐
☐
☐
☐
☐
☐
☐
☐
☐
☐

⌛
3min 30sec

Answers
on page 166

A

—

B

—

C

—

D

—

E

1 | 2 | 3 | 4 | 5

Fresh Powder

Slalom through these bumps
before the lift closes

13
changes

- - - - - - - -

KEEP
SCORE

☐
☐
☐
☐
☐
☐
☐
☐
☐
☐
☐
☐
☐

⧗

3min 40sec

Answers
on page 166

A

—

B

—

C

—

D

—

E

1 | 2 | 3 | 4 | 5

Gimme Shelter

If they can put together their tent, you can find the alterations we've made

A
—
B
—
C
—
D
—
E

1   2   3   4   5

9
changes

⏳

3min 45sec

Answers
on page 167

KEEP SCORE ★ ☐ ☐ ☐ ☐ ☐ ☐ ☐ ☐ ☐

The Magic Bus

Join these merry pranksters on their mystery tour

11
changes

- - - - - - - - -

KEEP
SCORE

❏
❏
❏
❏
❏
❏
❏
❏
❏
❏
❏

⧗

3min 55sec

Answers
on page 167

Surf's Up

You'll have a beach of a time figuring out what's unusual here

14
changes

KEEP
SCORE

A

B

C

D

E

⧗

3min 40sec

Answers
on page 167

1   2   3   4   5

Table for Four

Eat, drink, and spot the differences

A
—
B
—
C
—
D
—
E

1 | 2 | 3 | 4 | 5

13
changes

KEEP
SCORE

3min 20sec

Answers
on page 167

Into the Wild

What sort of highland high jinks are going on in this scenic snap?

A

B

C

D

E

1   2   3   4   5

10 changes

⧗

3min 15sec

Answers on page 167

KEEP SCORE ★ ❑ ❑ ❑ ❑ ❑ ❑ ❑ ❑ ❑ ❑

Beyond the Pail

Which one of these sunny photos has changed?
Find it, and you'll get a star.

1

2

3

4

5

6

0min 15sec

Answer
on page 167

A Dino-mite Duo

It won't take an archaeologist to unearth
the picture that's unlike the others

1

2

3

4

5

6

0min 25sec

Answer
on page 167

In the Attic

Reshuffle the gear, and you'll be ready to skedaddle

KEEP SCORE

⧖

0min 30sec

Answer
on page 167

Bargain Hunting

Try to find order in this outdoor bazaar

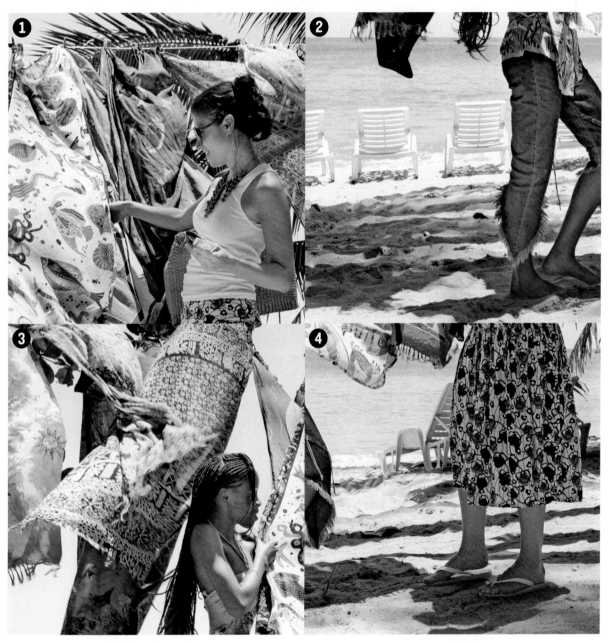

0min 40sec

Answer
on page 167

Roof Rack Required

Solving this brain-teaser is a lot like packing a car:
Everything's got to fit

A

B

C

D

E

1   2   3   4   5

11
changes

⧖

4min 20sec

Answers
on page 167

KEEP SCORE ★ ❑ ❑ ❑ ❑ ❑ ❑ ❑ ❑ ❑ ❑ ❑

Have Poncho, Will Travel

These cheerful vacationers are prepared for anything

A —

B —

C —

D —

E —

1   2   3   4   5

13
changes

KEEP
SCORE

❏
❏
❏
❏
❏
❏
❏
❏
❏
❏
❏
❏

⌛

4min 30sec

Answers
on page 168

Sitting Pretty

Now if only she were reading our book

A
—
B
—
C
—
D
—
E

1   2   3   4   5

10
changes

⧗

4min 40sec

Answers
on page 168

KEEP SCORE ★ ❏ ❏ ❏ ❏ ❏ ❏ ❏ ❏ ❏ ❏

A Canny Carny

Everyone's a winner.
Care to try your luck?

A

B

C

D

E

1   2   3   4   5

10
changes
- - - - - - - - -
KEEP
SCORE

❏
❏
❏
❏
❏
❏
❏
❏
❏
❏

⧗

4min 55sec

Answers
on page 168

Having a Ball

This one is as easy as
rolling down a hill

A

B

C

D

E

1   2   3   4   5

13
changes

⧗

4min 40sec

Answers
on page 168

KEEP SCORE ★ ❑ ❑ ❑ ❑ ❑ ❑ ❑ ❑ ❑ ❑ ❑ ❑ ❑

Cheers

They're willing to take a shot. Are you?

9
changes

- - - - - - - - -

KEEP
SCORE

❏
❏
❏
❏
❏
❏
❏
❏
❏

⧗

3min 25sec

Answers
on page 168

A

—

B

—

C

—

D

—

E

1   2   3   4   5

Local Knowledge

Let this boy be your guide

A
—
B
—
C
—
D
—
E

1 | 2 | 3 | 4 | 5

9
changes

- - - - - - - -

KEEP
SCORE

☐
☐
☐
☐
☐
☐
☐
☐
☐

⧗

3min 40sec

Answers
on page 168

Splish, Splash

Just when you thought it was safe
to go back in the water

A
—
B
—
C
—
D
—
E

1   2   3   4   5

11 changes

⏳

4min **15**sec

Answers
on page 168

KEEP SCORE ★ ☐ ☐ ☐ ☐ ☐ ☐ ☐ ☐ ☐ ☐ ☐

Ain't It Grand?

Follow these river rats through a shifting landscape

12
changes

KEEP
SCORE

5min 5sec

Answers
on page 168

MAST

ER[ ]

Here, puzzles get
a little harder. You'll
need to raise
your game a level.

A Bridge Too Far

Keep going because
you can't turn back now

A
–
B
–
C
–
D
–
E

1 | 2 | 3 | 4 | 5

8
changes

⧗

4min 40sec

Answers
on page 168

KEEP SCORE ★ ❑ ❑ ❑ ❑ ❑ ❑ ❑ ❑

Gliding Into Winter

Your reward will be a blazing hearth at the inn

A
—
B
—
C
—
D
—
E

1 | 2 | 3 | 4 | 5

10
changes

⧗
5min 10sec

Answers
on page 168

KEEP SCORE ★ ❑ ❑ ❑ ❑ ❑ ❑ ❑ ❑ ❑ ❑

The Golden Palace

Who's photographing the photographer? It's quite a stumper.

A

B

C

D

E

1 | 2 | 3 | 4 | 5

11
changes

KEEP
SCORE

⌛
4min **45**sec

Answers
on page 169

Smokin'

There will be hot times at the old lagoon tonight

12
changes

4min 50sec

Answers
on page 169

KEEP SCORE ★ ❏ ❏ ❏ ❏ ❏ ❏ ❏ ❏ ❏ ❏ ❏ ❏

MASTER

Painted Ponies Go Up and Down

In one of these pictures, something has malfunctioned

1

2

3

4

5

6

0min 40sec

Answer
on page 169

Flying the Friendly Skies

Which aerial view isn't quite like the others?

1

2

3

4

5

6

0min 45sec

Answer
on page 169

Win One for the Skipper

But first you have to put your oar in

A

B

C

D

E

1　　2　　3　　4　　5

11
changes

KEEP
SCORE

❑
❑
❑
❑
❑
❑
❑
❑
❑
❑
❑

⧗

5min 15sec

Answers
on page 169

A Roof With a View

It's amazing how a landscape can change in the blink of an eye

A
—
B
—
C
—
D
—
E

1 | 2 | 3 | 4 | 5

11
changes

5min 20sec

Answers
on page 169

KEEP SCORE ★ ☐ ☐ ☐ ☐ ☐ ☐ ☐ ☐ ☐ ☐ ☐

Smile for the Camera

This lad and lass are happy to oblige

A
—
B
—
C
—
D
—
E

1 | 2 | 3 | 4 | 5

13
changes

KEEP
SCORE
❑
❑
❑
❑
❑
❑
❑
❑
❑
❑
❑
❑
❑

⧗
5min 25sec

Answers
on page 169

Watch That First Step

Everyone's snap-happy on this tarmac

11
changes

KEEP
SCORE

❑
❑
❑
❑
❑
❑
❑
❑
❑
❑
❑

⏳

4min 35sec

Answers
on page 169

A

—

B

—

C

—

D

—

E

1 | 2 | 3 | 4 | 5

A Guided Journey

Sometimes even the most intrepid travelers need a little help

A

—

B

—

C

—

D

—

E

1 | 2 | 3 | 4 | 5

10
changes

KEEP
SCORE

4min 45sec

Answers
on page 169

Umbrella Group

These tourists may have to come again another day, but you won't

A
—
B
—
C
—
D
—
E

1 | 2 | 3 | 4 | 5

14
changes

⧗

5min **35**sec

Answers
on page 169

KEEP SCORE ★ ❑ ❑ ❑ ❑ ❑ ❑ ❑ ❑ ❑ ❑ ❑ ❑ ❑ ❑

Checkout Time

While they wait, you can put them in their proper places

1min 25sec

Answer
on page 170

KEEP SCORE

Let There Be Light

Help her illuminate this picture

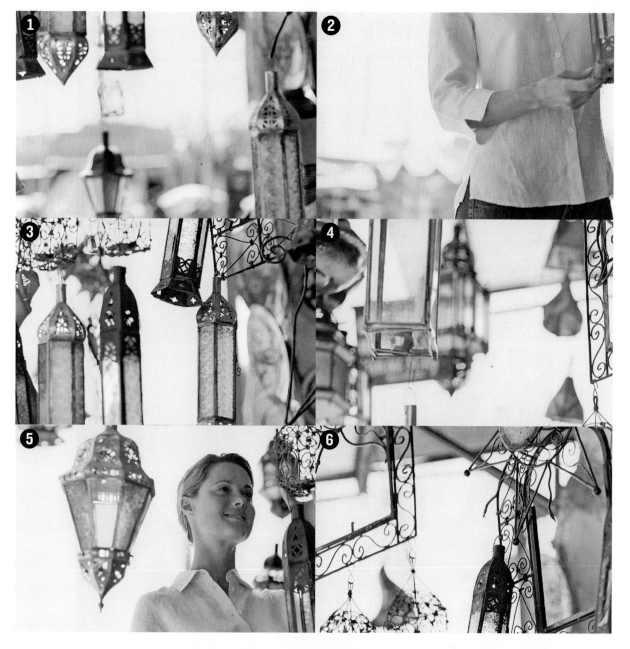

KEEP SCORE

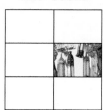

1min 15sec

Answer
on page 170

Ladies of the Canyon

These women are masters of their domain

A
—
B
—
C
—
D
—
E

1 | 2 | 3 | 4 | 5

14
changes

KEEP
SCORE

❏
❏
❏
❏
❏
❏
❏
❏
❏
❏
❏
❏
❏
❏

⏳

5min 30sec

Answers
on page 170

Desert Dining

When you lunch at the big tepee,
leave a big tip

A
—
B
—
C
—
D
—
E

1 | 2 | 3 | 4 | 5

14 changes

⧗
5min 20sec

Answers
on page 170

KEEP SCORE ★ ❏ ❏ ❏ ❏ ❏ ❏ ❏ ❏ ❏ ❏ ❏ ❏ ❏ ❏

A Leaf Peeper's Paradise

You'll fall for this puzzle

A
—
B
—
C
—
D
—
E

1   2   3   4   5

12
changes

⏳
4min **50**sec

Answers
on page 170

KEEP SCORE ★ ☐☐☐☐☐☐☐☐☐☐☐☐

Hang On Tight

This ride could be one you'll never forget

5 4 3 2 1

A B C D E

14
changes

KEEP
SCORE

❏ ❏ ❏ ❏ ❏ ❏ ❏ ❏ ❏ ❏ ❏ ❏ ❏ ❏

5min 15sec

Answers
on page 170

Hello, Comrade

She aspires to capture the spires with her cell phone

12
changes

KEEP
SCORE

A

—

B

—

C

—

D

—

E

4min 45sec

Answers
on page 170

1 | 2 | 3 | 4 | 5

Lonely Planet

Can you find the shortcut to Grindavík?

12
changes

- - - - - - - -

KEEP
SCORE

❏
❏
❏
❏
❏
❏
❏
❏
❏
❏
❏
❏

⌛

4min 40sec

Answers
on page 170

Walk Like an Egyptian

Tut-tut on you if you can't solve this riddle of the Sphinx

A

B

C

D

E

1 | 2 | 3 | 4 | 5

12
changes

⧗
4min 50sec

Answers
on page 170

KEEP SCORE ★ ❏ ❏ ❏ ❏ ❏ ❏ ❏ ❏ ❏ ❏ ❏ ❏

Roadside Respite

You've got it made in the shade

A
—
B
—
C
—
D
—
E

1 | 2 | 3 | 4 | 5

15
changes
- - - - - - - -
KEEP
SCORE

❏
❏
❏
❏
❏
❏
❏
❏
❏
❏
❏
❏
❏
❏
❏

⧗

5min 35sec

Answers
on page 171

A Tight Squeeze

Please keep your hands inside (and your eyes on) the boat

A
–
B
–
C
–
D
–
E

1 | 2 | 3 | 4 | 5

10
changes

4min **30**sec

Answers
on page 171

KEEP SCORE ★ ❑ ❑ ❑ ❑ ❑ ❑ ❑ ❑ ❑ ❑

Ah, the Spa Life!

One of our resorts is just a wee bit different

2min 20sec

Answer
on page 171

You Are What You Eat

Every day, lunch is the same—or is it?

1

2

3

4

5

6

1min 55sec

Answer
on page 171

Dog Day Afternoon

Hounds deserve a holiday too

KEEP SCORE ★ ❑ ❑ ❑ ❑ ❑ ❑ ❑ ❑ ❑ ❑ ❑ ❑ ❑ ❑ ❑ ❑

14
changes

⧗

5min 25sec

Answers
on page 171

Wish You Were Here

Actually, we wish *we* were here

16 changes

- - - - - - - -

KEEP SCORE

☐ ☐ ☐ ☐ ☐ ☐ ☐ ☐ ☐ ☐ ☐ ☐ ☐ ☐ ☐ ☐

⌛

5min 55sec

Answers on page 171

A — B — C — D — E

1 — 2 — 3 — 4 — 5

EXPE

RT [

Only serious puzzlers
dare to tread past this point.
Who's in?
]

On Top of the World

Some people find adventure thrilling;
others find it puzzling

A
—
B
—
C
—
D
—
E

1 | 2 | 3 | 4 | 5

14
changes

4min 55sec

Answers
on page 171

KEEP SCORE ★ ❏ ❏ ❏ ❏ ❏ ❏ ❏ ❏ ❏ ❏ ❏ ❏ ❏ ❏

The Fab Four

The faster you rush through this Rushmore riddle,
the rockier the outcome will be

A

B

C

D

E

1   2   3   4   5

13
changes

KEEP
SCORE
☐ ☐ ☐ ☐ ☐ ☐ ☐ ☐ ☐ ☐ ☐ ☐ ☐

⧗

4min 45sec

Answers
on page 171

Is Everybody Happy?

Tonight we're going to party like it's the year 24762549

14
changes

5min 5sec

Answers
on page 171

KEEP SCORE ★ ❏ ❏ ❏ ❏ ❏ ❏ ❏ ❏ ❏ ❏ ❏ ❏ ❏ ❏

Playing the Odds

Your chances here are better than even

11
changes

KEEP
SCORE

❑
❑
❑
❑
❑
❑
❑
❑
❑
❑
❑

⧗

4min 50sec

Answers
on page 172

Sandy Surrealism

We've taken this tricky building to a new level of distraction

A
—
B
—
C
—
D
—
E

1   2   3   4   5

17 changes

⧗

5min 30sec

Answers
on page 172

KEEP SCORE ★ ❑❑❑❑❑❑❑❑❑❑❑❑❑❑❑❑❑❑

Tools of the Trade

This sporty snapshot is game for anything

1

2

3

4

5

6

2min 40sec

Answer
on page 172

Where's My Beach Blanket?

One of these pictures is just a shade different

1

2

3

4

5

6

2min 15sec

Answer
on page 172

A Plague of Pigeons

This one's for the birds

A

B

C

D

E

1   2   3   4   5

14
changes

KEEP
SCORE

❏
❏
❏
❏
❏
❏
❏
❏
❏
❏
❏
❏
❏
❏

⧗

5min 5sec

Answers
on page 172

Great Walls of China!

The quiet and solitary puzzler apprehends the inscrutable.
Patience is needed.

17
changes

5min 50sec

Answers
on page 172

KEEP SCORE ★ ❑❑❑❑❑❑❑❑❑❑❑❑❑❑❑❑❑❑❑❑

On the Waterfront

The people along this canal are a changeable lot

15
changes

KEEP
SCORE

❏
❏
❏
❏
❏
❏
❏
❏
❏
❏
❏
❏
❏
❏
❏

⌛

5min 40sec

Answers
on page 172

Slanted View

Pinpointing the variations between these photos will hardly be a Pisa cake

15
changes
- - - - - - - -
KEEP
SCORE

❏
❏
❏
❏
❏
❏
❏
❏
❏
❏
❏
❏
❏
❏
❏

⧗

5min 35sec

Answers
on page 172

Where's My Prince?

That's one lucky … whatever it is

12
changes

KEEP
SCORE

⌛
4min 35sec

Answers
on page 172

A
–
B
–
C
–
D
–
E

1 | 2 | 3 | 4 | 5

Not From Around Here

Hint: Big Ben is behind you.
After that, you're on your own.

14
changes

KEEP
SCORE

⏳

4min 40sec

Answers
on page 173

A Leap of Faith

They're going for it, and so should you

17
changes
- - - - - - - - -
KEEP
SCORE

❏ ❏ ❏ ❏ ❏ ❏ ❏ ❏ ❏ ❏ ❏ ❏ ❏ ❏ ❏ ❏ ❏

⌛
5min 55sec

Answers
on page 173

Rush Hour

Are we there yet? *Are we there yet?*

A
—
B
—
C
—
D
—
E

1   2   3   4   5

13
changes

5min 10sec

KEEP SCORE ★ ❑ ❑ ❑ ❑ ❑ ❑ ❑ ❑ ❑ ❑ ❑ ❑ ❑

Answers
on page 173

Quite a Yarn

Tie up this tangle before everything unravels

A

B

C

D

E

1 | 2 | 3 | 4 | 5

16
changes

KEEP
SCORE

❏
❏
❏
❏
❏
❏
❏
❏
❏
❏
❏
❏
❏
❏
❏

⏳
6min 10sec

Answers
on page 173

Signs of Madness

These billboards look scarier than the Bates Motel

17
changes

KEEP
SCORE

❑
❑
❑
❑
❑
❑
❑
❑
❑
❑
❑
❑
❑
❑
❑
❑
❑

⏳

5min 20sec

Answers
on page 173

A

—

B

—

C

—

D

—

E

1   2   3   4   5

Slip Into Something Comfortable

Think they have anything in a size 14EEE?

13
changes
- - - - - - - -
KEEP
SCORE

❑
❑
❑
❑
❑
❑
❑
❑
❑
❑
❑
❑
❑

⌛

5min 5sec

Answers
on page 173

Enchanted Cottage

Here's a picture-perfect postcard—almost

17
changes
- - - - - - - - -
KEEP
SCORE

6min 15sec

Answers
on page 173

GENI

JS[

Finding a single difference in these puzzles is a challenge. Finding them all might be impossible.

]

Bite of the Apple

If you can solve it here, you can solve it anywhere

A
—
B
—
C
—
D
—
E

1   2   3   4   5

17
changes

⧖
6min **55**sec

Answers
on page 173

KEEP SCORE ★ ❑❑❑❑❑❑❑❑❑❑❑❑❑❑❑❑❑❑

Man Overboard

Okay, that one's easy. Now find the others.

16
changes
- - - - - - - - -
KEEP
SCORE

7min 15sec

Answers
on page 174

1   2   3   4   5

A   B   C   D   E

Beachside Feast

Kick it old school with these hipsters from yesteryear

A

B

C

D

E

1   2   3   4   5

22
changes

KEEP
SCORE

❏
❏
❏
❏
❏
❏
❏
❏
❏
❏
❏
❏
❏
❏
❏
❏
❏
❏
❏
❏
❏
❏

⏳

7min 35sec

Answers
on page 174

No Contest

Ordinarily, we'd bet on the bike

A
–
B
–
C
–
D
–
E

1   2   3   4   5

20
changes

7min 55sec

Answers
on page 174

KEEP SCORE ★ ❏

Castle in the Sand

Imagine the pail and shovel this masterpiece required

19
changes
- - - - - - - - -
KEEP
SCORE

7min 45sec

Answers
on page 174

A

B

C

D

E

1

2

3

4

5

Tea and Sympathy

There's nothing like good old English hospitality

GENIUS

17
changes

- - - - - - -

KEEP
SCORE

❏
❏
❏
❏
❏
❏
❏
❏
❏
❏
❏
❏
❏
❏
❏
❏
❏

⧗

7min 20sec

Answers
on page 174

A

—

B

—

C

—

D

—

E

1   2   3   4   5

Hagglers' Haven

Work fast—these items are priced to move

A
—
B
—
C
—
D
—
E

1   2   3   4   5

16
changes

- - - - - - - -

KEEP
SCORE

☐
☐
☐
☐
☐
☐
☐
☐
☐
☐
☐
☐
☐
☐
☐
☐

⧗

7min 40sec

Answers
on page 174

Whatever Floats Your Boat

That's no minor liner out there

28
changes

KEEP
SCORE

1 2 3 4 5

10min 45sec

Answers
on page 175

A   B   C   D   E

LIFE
CLASS

ICS[

These puzzles were
specially created with
memorable photos
from the LIFE archives.

]

Anchors Aweigh

What's been reshuffled on this deck?

A
–
B
–
C
–
D
–
E

1 | 2 | 3 | 4 | 5

8
changes

⧗

5min 40sec

Answers
on page 175

KEEP SCORE ★ ❑ ❑ ❑ ❑ ❑ ❑ ❑ ❑

Motel California

A stay at this La-La Land establishment might leave you slightly scrambled

14
changes

KEEP
SCORE

⏳

5min 10sec

Answers
on page 175

A
—
B
—
C
—
D
—
E

1 | 2 | 3 | 4 | 5

Who's Minding the Shore?

Someone needs to keep an eye on the boat

A
—
B
—
C
—
D
—
E

1   2   3   4   5

9
changes

KEEP
SCORE

❏
❏
❏
❏
❏
❏
❏
❏
❏

⌛
4min 25sec

Answers
on page 175

Summer Shuffle

Find the flaws in this board game

A
—
B
—
C
—
D
—
E

1 | 2 | 3 | 4 | 5

12
changes

- - - - - - - - -

KEEP
SCORE

❏
❏
❏
❏
❏
❏
❏
❏
❏
❏
❏
❏

⧗

4min 45sec

Answers
on page 175

Up the Creek

Keeping pace with these canoeists is half the battle

A
—
B
—
C
—
D
—
E

1 | 2 | 3 | 4 | 5

11 changes

⧗

4min 50sec

Answers on page 175

KEEP SCORE ★ ❑ ❑ ❑ ❑ ❑ ❑ ❑ ❑ ❑ ❑ ❑

The Complete Camper

You just know we've left out something

5 | 4 | 3 | 2 | 1

19
changes

- - - - - - - - -

KEEP
SCORE

❑ ❑ ❑ ❑ ❑ ❑ ❑ ❑ ❑ ❑ ❑ ❑ ❑ ❑ ❑ ❑ ❑ ❑ ❑

⌛

5min 55sec

Answers
on page 175

A | B | C | D | E

Folding Their Tent

Before this family packs it in, discover the ways this trip has changed them

A
—
B
—
C
—
D
—
E

1   2   3   4   5

10
changes

4min 20sec

Answers
on page 175

Occidental Oasis

Be the first to jump right in

A

B

C

D

E

1   2   3   4   5

14
changes

⧗
4min 45sec

Answers
on page 176

KEEP SCORE ★ ❑ ❑ ❑ ❑ ❑ ❑ ❑ ❑ ❑ ❑ ❑ ❑ ❑ ❑

Suiteless in Seattle

Bridezillas needn't attempt this puzzle

17
changes

KEEP
SCORE

6min 20sec

Answers
on page 176

[ANSWERS]

Finished already? Let's see how you did.

[INTRODUCTION]

Page 3: A Day to Remember No. 1 (A3): The pile behind the gondola has gotten much taller. No. 2 (A4): The stone supports below the window have been stretched downward. Nos. 3 and 4 (B4): The gondolier will have a hard time steering the boat with a broken oar. Is that why he's hiding his fingers? No. 5 (B5 to C5): Those windows have swapped places. No. 6 (C4): There must be a barber on board because the man has had a little taken off the side. No. 7 (D1 to E1): The hook is on growth hormones. No. 8 (D2): That pile now rests above the stairs. No. 9 (D3): Love is timeless, especially when you've lost your watch.

[NOVICE]

Page 8: Virtual Vacation No. 1 (A1 to A5): The rug is surging forward. No. 2 (B1): One of those stripes has gotten a little bit thicker. No. 3 (B1 to B2): The postcard has been turned right side up. No. 4 (B3): Her toenails have been repainted. No. 5 (B3 to C3): She's flipped her legs. No. 6 (B4 to C4): Wow, those pants are really stretchy. No. 7 (B5 to C5): Bigger maps are easier to read. No. 8 (D2 to D4): Her hem has been let out. No. 9 (E3): The straw has taken a hike. No. 10 (E4 to E5): The table has been pulled back. No. 11 (E5): Let's hope she doesn't need any more sunblock.

Page 10: London Calling No. 1 (A2): The sign above the entrance has disappeared. No. 2 (A4): Dad's part has switched sides. No. 3 (B1 to B2): The inner arch is descending. No. 4 (B2): Mom's shirt is down two stripes. No. 5 (B3): The Beefeater's beard has become beefier. No. 6 (C2): Please look straight at the camera. No. 7 (C3): The letters on his chest have exchanged places. No. 8 (D3): The boy's shirt has sprouted more buttons. No. 9 (D4 to D5): So that's where J.R.R. Tolkien got the idea for his trilogy. No. 10 (E1): The blackbird is playing hide and seek. No. 11 (E3): *Aw.* He's put his arm around the Beefeater.

Page 12: Hello Mudduh, Hello Fadduh No. 1 (A1 to A5): Those kids are growing so fast, the roof of the bus had to be raised. No. 2 (A4): A safety light has been added. No. 3 (B1 to D1): Someone's been drinking his milk. No. 4 (B3): The boy behind the blonde is going into hiding. No. 5 (B5): Another bus window has been opened. No. 6 (B5 to C5): The redhead must be using Miracle-Gro on his 'fro. No. 7 (C1 to D1): The boy in the light blue shirt has misplaced his hand. No. 8 (C3): Blondie's hoodie has lost its cuff. Nos. 9 and 10 (C4): The sporty girl has taken a shine to Rusty, and the bottom panel of her tank top is on the rise. No. 11 (D1): His foot has developed a bad case of elephantiasis. No. 12 (D2): The girl in the green shirt has switched her capris for khakis. No. 13 (D5): Rusty's back on the right foot. No. 14 (E1): Who knows where the shadow went.

Page 14: It's All Downhill From Here No. 1 (A2 to A3): He's getting a big head. No. 2 (A3): The birch has taken cover behind the foliage. No. 3 (B3 to D3): My, that girl has blossomed. No. 4 (B3): Her sleeve is growing too. No. 5 (B5): The man has been stripped of his stripes. No. 6 (C1 to D2): The boy's bike has had a sex change. No. 7 (C4 to D4): The woman's mountain bike has become a big wheel. No. 8 (D3 to E3): He's tugged his pants down. No. 9 (D4 to D5): The soles of her sneakers have been whitened.

Page 16: A Vexing Veldt Nos. 1, 2, and 3 (A4): The giraffe is taller, its horns are larger, and its lips seem chattier. No. 4 (C1): Her ponytail has flip-flopped. No. 5 (C2): The lioness has inched closer to her prey. No. 6 (C2 to D2): The girl in the center has made like Rapunzel and let down her hair. No. 7 (C3): That gazelle should have looked before he leapt onto that spot. No. 8 (D3): The middle horse has gotten his head out of the grass. No. 9 (D5): The cuff of her jeans has been lowered a smidge.

Page 18: Everything's in the Trunk No. 1 (A1): The bird is soaring closer to the trees. No. 2 (B1): He's donning some slick shades. No. 3 (B4): The mahout has moved a little farther back on his elephant. No. 4 (C3 to D3): The rope securing their carriage has come undone. No. 5 (D2): A stone has been added to that statue. No. 6 (D4 to D5): The wall and the tree trunk have been removed to give them a better view of the lake. No. 7 (E1): If the elephant gets a gander of that mouse, their ride will come to a crashing end. No. 8 (E1 to E2): His front left leg is hovering. No. 9 (E4): And the other pachyderm has lost his. No. 10 (E5): Plus, he's curled his trunk in the other direction.

Page 20: Put the Lime in the Coconut No. 1 (A3 to A5): The palm fronds have flourished. No. 2 (B5): While money may not grow on trees, coconuts do. No. 3 (C1): Two more rows of tiles have been added to that wall. No. 4 (C1 to D1): And some of the tiles in the reflection have merged. No. 5 (D3): She's clipped the top bikini strap. Nos. 6 and 7 (D5): The lady in the ocean is in deeper water, and a palm frond has sprouted up. No. 8 (E1): Another flower has floated into the hot tub. No. 9 (E2 to E3): They've lost their seat. No. 10 (E5): A lime has landed in the coconut, so as the song says, they'll need to drink them both down.

Page 21: Fresh Powder No. 1 (A4): Judging by the reflection in his goggles, construction is booming in these parts. No. 2 (A4 to C5): Apparently, you're never too old for a growth spurt. No. 3 (B1 to C1): The window has become extra paneful. No. 4 (B2): The eave has been abbreviated. No. 5 (B3): Her goggles might flip you out. No. 6 (C2): The yellow stripe on her jacket has been removed. No. 7 (C3): The square on

her snowboard is whole again. No. 8 (C3 to E3): Those snow bunnies have gotten a little cozier. No. 9 (D2 to D3): The circle has been unbroken. No. 10 (D3): The red dot has slid up. No. 11 (D3 to D5): He can't hit the slopes without bindings. No. 12 (E1): The snow is inching up. No. 13 (E2): A logo has been tacked on her board.

Page 22: **Gimme Shelter** No. 1 (A3 to B3): Check out the bigger towel. Nos. 2 and 3 (B4): His hair has gotten shaggier, and he's no longer a man of peace. No. 4 (C1): She's mislaid part of the tent pole. No. 5 (C4): One of his bracelets has crept up his arm. No. 6 (C5): He's missing part of the pole as well. No. 7 (D3): His sandal has hoofed off. No. 8 (E2): She might have lost a pole, but she has gained a necklace. No. 9 (E5): Her boot is made for kicking.

Page 24: **The Magic Bus** No. 1 (A2 to A3): You can never have enough safety lights. No. 2 (A4 to A5): Someone must have fed that tree a megaton of fertilizer. No. 3 (B1): The door has been given an upgrade. No. 4 (B3): Guess the onboard computer doesn't have a spell-check. No. 5 (C1 to C2): That couple now has matching lenses. No. 6 (C2 to C3): The woman in the striped shirt has ditched her binoculars. No. 7 (C3): That guy needed to take a bathroom break. No. 8 (C4 to C5): Osteoporosis has done a number on the man in the green polo shirt. No. 9 (D5): And as he was shrinking, his watch must have fallen off. No. 10 (E1): Her sneaker has lost its sole. No. 11 (E3): If Labor Day has passed, she'll have to change her shoes one more time.

Page 26: **Surf's Up** No. 1 (A1 to B2): One of the palms is just a bit shorter. No. 2 (B1): The longer the boards, the better the surfing. No. 3 (B1 to B2): Someone has run off with the hearts of those palms. No. 4 (B4): One of the surfboards has lost its fin. No. 5 (C2): The rear door handle is missing. No. 6 (C4 to C5): That's quite a swell. No. 7 (C5): The fence post has shot up. No. 8 (D1 to E1): The exhaust pipe has disappeared. No. 9 (D2): The wheel well has been lowered. No. 10 (D2 to D3): The rear door looks snazzier with less trim. No. 11 (D3 to D4): While we're at it, let's lower the trim on the front door … No. 12 (D4): … and extend the trim above the wheel well … No. 13 (D5): … and beef up the bumper. No. 14 (E5): The sand by the front wheel has been swept away.

Page 27: **Table for Four** No. 1 (A3 to C3): Nothing's holding up the umbrella. No. 2 (A4): Dad's hair is not only going gray, it's receding. No. 3 (B4): Maybe he's trying to distract us from the hair situation with that earring. No. 4 (B4 to C5): Wasn't the waitress on the left before? No. 5 (C1 to D1): The boy has dropped his fork. No. 6 (C2): And Mom's fork is getting longer. No. 7 (C3): The lady sitting behind them must have taken a powder. No. 8 (C3 to C4): Those pink ponytail holders go well with her outfit. No. 9 (C4 to C5): The chair back has risen. No. 10 (D1): Now there is more room for food on the table. No. 11 (D2 to D3): The slice of lemon

has become an orange. No. 12 (D3): The lemonade has turned pink. No. 13 (E3 to E4): Her halter has shrunk into a bikini top.

Page 28: **Into the Wild** No. 1 (B4): The ewe is closing in for the kill. No. 2 (C1 to D1): The tent for two has become a tent for three. No. 3 (C3): The portable stove has gained a tier. Nos. 4, 5, and 6 (C4): The boy seems somewhat concerned. Maybe it's because his cup has turned red, and the juice bottle has grown taller—or it could be the ewe? No. 7 (C5): Who turned on the car lights? No. 8 (D2 to E4): The planks have merged. No. 9 (D3 to D4): His jacket has devoured his sweatshirt. No. 10 (E5): A table leg has hopped away.

Page 30: **Beyond the Pail** In photo No. 5, the rake has wandered off.

Page 31: **A Dino-mite Duo** You can see through the beast's skull in photo No. 1.

Page 32: **In the Attic**

4	2
1	3

Page 33: **Bargain Hunting**

3	1
2	4

Page 34: **Roof Rack Required** No. 1 (B2): The roof on the house is way pointier. No. 2 (B3): The antenna is in search of better reception. No. 3 (C1): At least that patch of grass is winning the war against concrete. No. 4 (C2): The driver-side door has been shut. No. 5 (C3): The trunk lid has come unhinged on the right. Nos. 6 and 7 (C5): The fence will need mending, but that side of the lawn now has less grass to mow. Nos. 8 and 9 (D2): The basket has been truncated, and, yes, that license plate works for us. No. 10 (E2): The black suitcase is sliding closer to the car. No. 11 (E3 to E4): The sunglasses have tumbled off the cooler.

Page 36: Have Poncho, Will Travel No. 1 (B1): His hat is a trifle taller. Nos. 2 and 3 (B3): Her sunglasses are blushing, and one of the flowers on her blouse is now blue. No. 4 (C4): The lady next to her has lost her camera. No. 5 (C5): The guy on the right has moved his hand. No. 6 (D1): His socks have turned teal. No. 7 (D1 to E1): And he'd better watch his step. Nos. 8 and 9 (D2): Her poncho sleeve has been trimmed, thus revealing that the woman behind her has no right foot. No. 10 (D3): And our little miracle of science has no left foot, either. No. 11 (D3 to E3): Her pant legs have knit themselves together. No. 12 (D5): He's kicked off his sandal. No. 13 (E4): Her tote has been supersized.

Page 38: Sitting Pretty No. 1 (B3): The boat has caught a favorable wind. No. 2 (B5): The bush has gotten bushier. No. 3 (C1 to D1): Termites have attacked the left side of the fence. No. 4 (C5 to D5): A few slats on the love seat have ganged up. No. 5 (C5): That hat may not fit her anymore. No. 6 (D3): The white wrap has lost its fringe. No. 7 (D4): That's a pretty big diamond . . . on her pillow. No. 8 (E3): Her drink has turned a brighter shade of yellow. *Eww.* No. 9 (E4): She's had her toenails redone. No. 10 (E4 to E5): The coffee table has been given a new edge.

Page 40: A Canny Carny No. 1 (A1): Green before white is a friend of . . . Dwight? No. 2 (A3 to A4): The toy turtle's head has turned purple. No. 3 (C2): The Pteroil mascot has been demoted. No. 4 (C3 to C4): He can't wait for his shift to be over. No. 5 (C5): The comet has changed direction. No. 6 (D1): That critter seems bored. No. 7 (D2 to D4): The numbers have traded places. No. 8 (D2 to E2): The spiral is now spinning clockwise. No. 9 (E3 to E4): The red stripe has been narrowed. No. 10 (E5): The handle is in search of a better target.

Page 42: Having a Ball No. 1 (B1 to B2): What's Dad doing to keep that beach ball in place? No. 2 (B2): Whatever it is, maybe it'll also explain his sudden beard growth. No. 3 (B3): Mom's become a Breck girl. No. 4 (C2): Dad's trunks are lopsided. Nos. 5 and 6 (C3): The towel is more sizable, and Mom's gotten modest about her midriff. Nos. 7 and 8 (C4): The pendant's chain is broken, and the top of the hula hoop has vanished. No. 9 (C5): A bush has blown away. No. 10 (D3): That cooler handle will not prevail. No. 11 (D5): Sis has dropped her bucket. No. 12 (E4): A bloom on the boy's shorts is now totally orange. No. 13 (E5): One of the red dots on the girl's skirt has ballooned.

Page 44: Cheers No. 1 (A1 to B1): The menu board has expanded. No. 2 (A2): The waitress must have forgotten something. No. 3 (A3): The Sox logo has fallen. No. 4 (B1 to C1): Didn't you know that coconuts grow long after they've been picked? No. 5 (C2): He can't toast without a glass. Nos. 6 and 7 (C3): Make hers a double. And the chair next to the pole has lost a leg. No. 8 (D2 to E2): The coffee cup has angled its way between them. No. 9 (E4): Her bracelet has cloned itself.

Page 45: Local Knowledge No. 1 (A1 to B1): A minaret has joined the party. No. 2 (B2): Now all the girls have sunglasses. No. 3 (C2): The car has driven off. No. 4 (C4 to E5): Her nails have turned blue. No. 5 (D1 to D2): He's recrossed his arms. No. 6 (E1 to E2): And he's pulled down his shirt. No. 7 (E2): She's showing less leg. No. 8 (E3): She can write a longer note on a bigger postcard. No. 9 (E5): Her ring has a habit of hopping from one hand to the other.

Page 46: Splish, Splash No. 1 (A2): The plane has reached its destination. No. 2 (A3 to A4): More fronds have sprouted. No. 3 (A5): The umbrella has been kicked up a notch. No. 4 (B2): A plant has engulfed the tree trunk. No. 5 (B4): The boy's bangs have grown in. No. 6 (C2): The smiley face is expanding. No. 7 (C2 to C3): She's about to get Dad's attention. No. 8 (C5): The chair needs leg work. No. 9 (D2): What happened to her rubber ducky? Nos. 10 and 11 (D5): A row of bricks has disappeared, and a tiny shark has stopped in for a quick bite.

Page 48: Ain't It Grand? No. 1 (A4 to C5): The cliff on the right has been worn down. No. 2 (B3 to B4): But the sandstone bluff is gaining ground. No. 3 (C1): The black oar has a greater reach. No. 4 (C1 to C2): The red kayak has fallen back. No. 5 (C2 to E5): Almost the entire raft is but a mirror image of its former self. No. 6 (C2): The oar has turned completely blue. No. 7 (C3): They'll need to send out a search party for the orange kayak. No. 8 (C4): The blue kayak has been dyed red to match its oar. No. 9 (D2): His hat brim now offers serious sun protection. No. 10 (D2 to E3): And he's shimmied to the right. No. 11 (E1): Plus, he may want to fix his oar. No. 12 (E2): Spare glove, anyone?

[MASTER]

Page 52: A Bridge Too Far No. 1 (B3 to C3): The steeple has been given a lift. No. 2 (C1 to D2): She's gotten a step closer to her journey's end. No. 3 (C2): The post has been given a boost. No. 4 (C4): A window has rolled away. No. 5 (C5 to D5): A streetlamp is missing. No. 6 (D4 to D5): One of the ropes has disappeared. No. 7 (E2): The base of the bridge has shrunk. No. 8 (E3): The toy boat is sailing away.

Page 54: Gliding Into Winter No. 1 (A3 to B3): The wind is pushing the smoke in the other direction. Nos. 2 and 3 (B2): The windows have exchanged places, and an extra chimney has been added. No. 4 (B3): The bell tower has lost its support. No. 5 (B4): That house will be a lot smokier without a chimney. No. 6 (C1 to E2): The skier on the left is making some headway. No. 7 (C2): Another room has been illuminated. No. 8 (C4 to D4): The other skier is zipping along too. Nos. 9 and 10 (C5): Someone has shut the door to the house on the right, and the fence rail has been lengthened.

Page 56: The Golden Palace No. 1 (A1 to B2): The statue has been eating its Wheaties. No. 2 (A2): The moon is almost full. No. 3 (A3 to A4): The temple's uppermost spire looks stunted and tipsy. No. 4 (C2): A smaller spire on the bottom left has been sent out for polishing. No. 5 (C4): The lamp has been extinguished. No. 6 (D1 to E2): The statue's legs and feet have turned blue. No. 7 (D4 to D5): The shadow has been erased. No. 8 (E2): That pole has been trimmed. No. 9 (E2 to E3): And so, too, her ponytail. No. 10 (E3 to E4): A thief has made off with her bag. No. 11 (E4): Her bracelet is inching up her arm.

Page 58: Smokin' No. 1 (B2 to B3): More people have gone for a dip. No. 2 (B3 to C3): He is scanning the other side of the lagoon. No. 3 (B4): One of the metal bars has evaporated. No. 4 (B5): A swimmer has moved on. No. 5 (C2): The crag has reached a new height. No. 6 (C3): Has he turned vampiric? No. 7 (C3 to D4): The sign is taking a broader stance. No. 8 (C4): The slats have coalesced. No. 9 (C5): The pump has been pushed over the edge. No. 10 (D2): That rock is sallying forth. No. 11 (D3 to E4): It's beautiful when two boards become one. No. 12 (E2 to E3): Another twist has been added to the walkway.

Page 60: Painted Ponies Go Up and Down The pole below the pony on the far right has vanished from photo No. 6.

Page 61: Flying the Friendly Skies The back wheel in photo No. 4 has been filled with a lot more air.

Page 62: Win One for the Skipper No. 1 (A1): The new window lets in more light. No. 2 (A3 to B4): One dome has been reduced . . . No. 3 (A5 to B5): . . . while another has flown the coop. No. 4 (B1 to C1): The red piles have been stretched to accommodate extra-tall ships. No. 5 (B2): The flag has flapped away. No. 6 (B3 to C3): Another gondolier has rowed onto the scene. Nos. 7 and 8 (C4): The white boat with the red oars is drifting to the right, and longer paddles probably won't help the crew in the tiny craft. Nos. 9 and 10 (D2): Eyes lowered and grin apparent, that vessel looks happier and more relaxed. No. 11 (D2 to E4): You think those front-runners are taking steroids? Looks like their boat is too.

Page 64: A Roof With a View No. 1 (B4): The minarets on the right are standing taller. No. 2 (C1): Poor chap—he's starting to lose his hair. No. 3 (C2): That apartment building is known for its friendliness. No. 4 (C3): Two more little domes have cropped up.

Nos. 5 and 6 (D3): The exit has been sealed, and the back of one chair has been filled in. No. 7 (D4): His shirtsleeve has been lowered a stitch. Nos. 8 and 9 (D5): The table at the far right has been cleared and readied for two more customers. No. 10 (E2 to E3): The blue table is about to topple. No. 11 (E3): Another ashtray and sugar bowl have been set out.

Page 66: Smile for the Camera No. 1 (A1 to B1): The itsy-bitsy bricks move up the concrete wall. No. 2 (A2 to A5): The decorative ledges have been repainted. No. 3 (B2 to C3): The milk jug is now industrial size. No. 4 (B3): One little brick has vanished. No. 5 (B4): Another brick has spun to the left. No. 6 (B4 to C4): The old brass pot has reversed itself. No. 7 (B5): The back wall is suffering from a falling arch. No. 8 (B5 to C5): The pot has flipped over. No. 9 (C1 to E3): He's giving us a friendly salute. No. 10 (C3 to D3): That stump still has some life in it. No. 11 (C3 to C5): Four bricks have united. No. 12 (C5): The pipe has run away. No. 13 (D4): She's taken a cue from the title of this puzzle.

Page 68: Watch That First Step No. 1 (A1): Minus the floodlight, that section of the tarmac will be a lot darker. No. 2 (A2): The control tower is taller. No. 3 (A4): The handle has switched direction. No. 4 (A4 to C5): The stairway has disappeared. Nos. 5, 6, 7, and 8 (A5): Someone's in a hurry to deplane, and a window has been added to the aircraft, which has gained one passenger and lost another. No. 9 (B2 to B3): The tail wing has fallen off. No. 10 (B4): The wheel flap has earned an extra zero. No. 11 (C4 to D4): Only a great photographer can slide backward.

Page 69: A Guided Journey No. 1 (A2): Urban renewal often leads to window removal. No. 2 (A3 to A4): One of the lights beneath the awning has been taken down. No. 3 (B1): That storefront has gotten extra cool. Nos. 4 and 5 (B2): CAKE has swapped places with SHOP, and a Chinese character has been turned on its head. No. 6 (C2): He should have kept an eye on his watch. No. 7 (C3 to C4): That business has changed its phone number to something catchier. No. 8 (C4 to D4): She's tossed her tail. No. 9 (D1): The silver car is pulling out of its spot. No. 10 (E4): Her guide has gone from TOP to POP.

Page 70: Umbrella Group No. 1 (B3 to C3): The middle spire is now almost level with the others. No. 2 (B4): Palm tree, begone! No. 3 (C1 to C2): The two ladies on the left have swapped heads. No. 4 (C1 to D1): And the woman in pink has lost her pass. No. 5 (C2): The person lingering in the temple doorway must have gone inside. No. 6 (C3): With a busted shaft, the green umbrella will likely fly off its handle. No. 7 (C4): What's caught his eye? No. 8 (C5): Her hat's off. No. 9 (D1): A bald guy has snuck up behind the lady in the striped shirt. No. 10 (D2): The monk has unfurled his robes. No. 11 (D3 to E3): His pennant has turned red. Nos. 12 and 13 (E2): Her capris have been lengthened, and the soles of her shoes have turned blue. No. 14 (E4): He's mastered the art of levitation.

Page 72: Checkout Time

3	6
2	5
1	4

Page 73: Let There Be Light

4	6
5	3
2	1

Page 74: Ladies of the Canyon
No. 1 (A1 to B1): The top of her ski has been pared down. No. 2 (A3 to C3): The waterfall's gush is not as flush. No. 3 (B3): The red boot has become a high-top. No. 4 (B4 to C4): That cliff looks like it's about to explode. No. 5 (C2 to D2): The incredible shrinking ski has also said sayonara to its bottom blade. Nos. 6 and 7 (D1 to E1): She's straining to get a better foothold now that her pole has lost its position. No. 8 (D2 to E2): And her other ski has gotten longer. No. 9 (D4 to D5): The top of the redhead's pole has run for the hills. No. 10 (D5): And the label on her ski has followed suit. No. 11 (D5 to E5): Plus, she's swung her arm out of view. Nos. 12 and 13 (E3): The blonde has grown pigtails and tucked the end of her friend's blade under her arm. No. 14 (E4 to E5): All that climbing has triggered a small landslide.

Page 76: Desert Dining
No. 1 (A2 to B2): The rock face is moving forward. No. 2 (A3 to A4): The tent poles have bloomed. No. 3 (C5): A few more bushes have cropped up. No. 4 (D1 to D2): The letters on that sign have been repainted red. No. 5 (D2): This eating establishment AIN'T afraid of slang. No. 6 (D2 to E2): The guy in the T-shirt has gotten higher. No. 7 (D3): Where's the medicine man? No. 8 (D3 to D4): A window has been added to this wigwam. No. 9 (D4): A bison has stormed onto the mural. No. 10 (E1): The red Trans Am has been given an awfully funny racing stripe. Nos. 11, 12, and 13 (E3): Someone has switched the license plate on the red sedan, jacked its tire, and turned two triangles into one. No. 14 (E4): Lunch here has become a bit pricey.

Page 78: A Leaf Peeper's Paradise
No. 1 (B1): The chimney on the left is on a slow skyward crawl. Nos. 2 and 3 (B2): The other smokestack has moved to the right, and a new window has been tacked on the second floor. No. 4 (B4 to B5): One of the tree's bottom limbs has been sawed off. No. 5 (B5): The pole is shooting up. No. 6 (C1): Someone has hung the yellow mums on the back stairs. No. 7 (C2): A pot of begonias has taken the mums' old spot. Nos. 8 and 9 (C4): The scarecrow is staring directly at us, while the owners are *test*ing out that entrance. Nos. 10 and 11 (C5): The letters on the sign in the background have been reversed, and now there's no room at this B&B. No. 12 (D2 to E2): Please don't eat the kale.

Page 80: Hang On Tight
No. 1 (A1 to A2): The posts have been raised. No. 2 (A1 to B1): A car has rocketed into view. No. 3 (A3): Part of the track has ruptured. No. 4 (A4 to A5): Two beams have been removed. No. 5 (A5): The remote-controlled airplane has blown up. No. 6 (A5 to B5): CHILLS has been placed before THRILLS. No. 7 (B5): The yellow submarine's periscope has acquired a better view. No. 8 (C1): The letter *A* has been flipped upside down. No. 9 (C4): The girl has gotten an extra scoop. No. 10 (C4 to C5): Talk about quick-drying nail polish. No. 11 (C5): The porthole on the right now matches its buddy on the left. No. 12 (D1 to E1): The top of the gate has become quite solid. No. 13 (D5): An *E* has been excised. No. 14 (E5): The stripes have turned red.

Page 82: Hello, Comrade
No. 1 (A4 to B4): The top of the cathedral is ascending to heaven. No. 2 (B2 to C2): If she wants to take a picture, she'll need to retrieve the top of her cell phone. No. 3 (C4 to D4): The green-and-red dome has been reversed. Nos. 4 and 5 (D3): A cloud bank has enveloped the back tower, and workers have bricked up the middle arch beneath the green-and-yellow dome. No. 6 (D4): Two windows are better than one. No. 7 (E1): She's pulled down her sweater. Nos. 8 and 9 (E2): The air-conditioning unit atop the office building and the ventilation slats above the windows have doubled. No. 10 (E3): That couple is moving farther apart. No. 11 (E4): The sculptural warrior has dropped his shield. No. 12 (E5): A tree grows in Moscow.

Page 83: Lonely Planet
No. 1 (B1 to C1): Hey, ewe—get b*aaa*ck to where you once belonged. No. 2 (B1 to C3): The mountain is sporting a larger profile. No. 3 (C1 to C3): The sign has headed closer to town. Nos. 4 and 5 (C2): Grindavík has moved three kilometers down the road and changed the spelling of its name. No. 6 (C3 to C4): The highway numbers have swapped places. No. 7 (C4 to D5): Keflavík's sign has grown. Nos. 8 and 9 (C4): The town has traded its airport for an aquarium and, by decree, flipped the *E* in its name. No. 10 (D3): One of the posts has vanished. No. 11 (D3 to D4): A miracle bush has sprouted from the concrete. No. 12 (D5): Another post has cracked up.

Page 84: Walk Like an Egyptian
No. 1 (A4 to B4): The ancients always said the Sphinx was a late bloomer. No. 2 (B2 to C3): So, of course, the pyramid behind it feels smaller. No. 3 (C1): Many more people have joined that expedition party. Nos. 4 and 5 (C5): Another group of tourists has appeared on the horizon, and that camel is galloping along. No. 6 (D1): The woman in the blue cap is catching up to the guy in the brown vest. No. 7 (D2): The man in the blue shirt has put his hand on his hip. No. 8 (D3): Her shorts have been cropped. No. 9 (D3 to E3): That backpacker has had one too many Big Macs. No. 10 (E2): The gal in the blue cap has a twin. No. 11 (E2 to E3): The lady in the white T-shirt is casting a larger shadow. No. 12 (D4 to E4): The woman in the blue and the guy in the yellow have stepped aside in unison.

Page 86: Roadside Respite No. 1 (B1): One of the trees has bloomed. No. 2 (C1 to C4): The roof has gotten a raise. No. 3 (C4): Two green stripes on the awning have merged. No. 4 (C5): The light has swiveled to the right. No. 5 (D1 to E1): The concrete is slowly overtaking the grass. No. 6 (D2): The coffee cup has been widened. Nos. 7, 8, and 9 (D3): The woman in the yellow dress has lost her shadow, the guy in the white shirt has put on a bow tie, and the electrical outlet has moved to higher ground. No. 10 (D3 to D4): Her tank top is down a stripe. Nos. 11 and 12 (D4): The guy in the glasses has been cloned, and the wheel on the green station wagon has rolled away. No. 13 (D5): The white stripe is reaching out. No. 14 (E1 to E2): Her chair doesn't seem all that supportive. No. 15 (E5): The pole has been shortened.

Page 88: A Tight Squeeze No. 1 (A1): Did the blimp lose some air? No. 2 (C1 to C2): The sun umbrella has taken off. No. 3 (C2): The yellow pole has been elevated. Nos. 4 and 5 (C3): The horn is higher, and the bald guy has left the deck. No. 6 (C4): The car is getting closer to the edge. No. 7 (D2 to D3): The trim has turned red. No. 8 (D3 to E3): An extra row of portholes has been added. No. 9 (D4): The embankment has been fortified with another stone. No. 10 (E1): One of the many begging bass that live in this river has made an appearance.

Page 90: Ah, the Spa Life! In photo No. 3, the first bend in the rock garden has been widened.

Page 91: You Are What You Eat Beware the vendor in photo No. 5—he's lost his license.

Page 92: Dog Day Afternoon No. 1 (A1 to B3): The umbrella has shifted down ever so slightly. Nos. 2 and 3 (B1): The top of the pine has come into view, and the bottle has pulled a 180. No. 4 (B4 to B5): The attic has become a little more spacious. No. 5 (C1 to D1): The yellow lab is getting a closer sniff of the hound's back paws. No. 6 (C2 to D2): The Boston terrier is off the leash. Nos. 7 and 8 (C3): With his new and improved ears, that Malinois can hear the black lab creeping up on him. No. 9 (C3 to C4): A German shepherd has joined the party. No. 10 (C4): The spiral topiary near the porch needs to be trimmed. No. 11 (C5): The top shadow on the middle fence post has straightened itself out. No. 12 (D4): The lime wedge has switched rims. Nos. 13 and 14 (E4): The wineglass on the right has lost half its stem, and Sherlock has struck a different pose.

Page 94: Wish You Were Here No. 1 (A1): The umbrella's blue flap has blown away. No. 2 (B2): A spoke is missing. No. 3 (B5): A section of the other bumbershoot's shaft has been cut out. No. 4 (C1): A man has wandered onto the shore. No. 5 (C2): The boat has changed direction. Nos. 6, 7, and 8 (C3): The guy in the white cap has trained his binoculars on the skiff that has gone adrift, and the islet along the horizon has switched sides. Nos. 9 and 10 (C4): Another boat has sailed in, and a second girl is there to greet it. Nos. 11 and 12 (C5): That speedboat is moving closer inland because the tide is high on that patch of sand. No. 13 (D2 to D3): The chair has become stripier. No. 14 (D5): You never know when you'll need a spare sandal. No. 15 (E1 to E2): The bar has burrowed itself beneath the sand. No. 16 (E4): Someone must be liking LIFE.

[EXPERT]

Page 98: On Top of the World No. 1 (A1 to A5): The mountain range has been put in reverse. No. 2 (B1): The bottom of the sherpa's scarf has flown off. Nos. 3 and 4 (B1 to C1): Off in the distance, a rider and his guide have moved closer to the rest of the group, and another explorer has joined them. Nos. 5 and 6 (B3 to C3): The air up there has enhanced her hair, while the guy next to her has vanished. Nos. 7 and 8 (C1): His boots have gained a stripe, and the woman in front of him has lost her ability to rein. No. 9 (C5 to E5): Those two horses have fallen back from the pack. No. 10 (D3): She's got legging, and she knows how to use it. No. 11 (D4): A patch of grass has pulled up its roots. No. 12 (E2): Maybe it moved over here. No. 13 (E3): A leg has hoofed off. No. 14 (E5): The boot is suddenly blue.

Page 100: The Fab Four No. 1 (A2 to B4): Now we have proof that Lincoln coveted Washington's place in history. No. 2 (B1 to B2): The eagle has turned. No. 3 (B1 to C2): The emblem on the monument's flag has completely changed its point of view. No. 4 (C4): The pole on the right has become a bit plainer. Nos. 5 and 6 (C5): The first N in WISCONSIN has gone Cyrillic, which seems to have caused the flag to hang a little lower. No. 7 (D2): That coin-op machine needs to cut back on the quarters. No. 8 (E1): The viewer has lost its base. Nos. 9, 10, and 11 (E3): He has pulled down his sweatshirt, while she has pulled up her left-hand sock, and one of the black checks on her jacket has been reddened. No. 12 (E4 to E5): A rail has been added to that section of the fence. No. 13 (E5): The post's stature has increased.

Page 102: Is Everybody Happy? Nos. 1 and 2 (A2): The 6 has become a 9, and one of the tassels has chosen a different path. No. 3 (A4): Beavers have made a snack of that pole. No. 4 (B1): Another tassel is missing. Nos. 5 and 6 (B5 to C5): The skyscraper has reached a new low, while the gold foil has worked its way up the column. No. 7 (C2): The construction crane must have found a new roost. No. 8 (C3): The streetlamp has lost its balance. No. 9 (C4 to D4): Hey, buddy, no cutting in line. No. 10 (C5): Yeah, we all need some column we can lean on. No. 11 (C5 to D5): Who drank the water? No. 12 (D2): A rail has been plucked from the barrier. No. 13 (E1): His socks have shrunk. No. 14 (E3): And that guy has switched to capris. How fashion forward.

Page 104: Playing the Odds Nos. 1 and 2 (A1 to A5): The top of this one-armed bandit has been downsized, and the deep purple drops at the upper corners have been lightened. No. 3 (A2 to A4): They'll have to change the name to Quintuple Diamonds. No. 4 (B2 to C4): All the payouts except for the top two have been switched. No. 5 (C1 to C4): The keypad and the digital readout have swapped places. No. 6 (C4): The display type at the bottom of the payout list has developed a stutter. No. 7 (D2): Does a *rar* trump a bar? No. 8 (D3): Taking a spin on this slot machine just got a lot more expensive. Nos. 9 and 10 (D4 to D5): Obviously, it's 10 times better to be a PAID WINNER. No. 11 (D5): An *E* has dropped out of the game.

Page 106: Sandy Surrealism No. 1 (A2 to A3): The top flag has found a new direction. No. 2 (B1): And the banner on the far left now flies for LIFE. Nos. 3 and 4 (B4): Both the pennant and the streetlight have been revived. No. 5 (B4 to B5): Could it have something to do with the length the lamp's neck has reached? No. 6 (C2 to C4): The trompe l'oeil's trim has banded together. No. 7 (C3): That new window certainly stands out. No. 8 (C4): A cop has just been assigned to that beat. No. 9 (C5): The glass has gone from plain to stained. No. 10 (D1): The Porta-John is popular spot with the gents. No. 11 (D2): That lady might be a little flat, but she moves gracefully. No. 12 (D3): Another turn-of-the-century dame has made her debut. No. 13 (D4): The view from that corner has become transparent. No. 14 (D5): The picture has been enlarged. Nos. 15, 16, and 17 (E3): The beach umbrella gives new meaning to the term *burnt orange,* the cooler is inching toward the sea, and his sock is on the rise.

Page 108: Tools of the Trade In photo No. 3, the creel has reeled in a fish.

Page 109: Where's My Beach Blanket? The long and lean lad in the top corner has taken a little jump to the left in photo No. 5.

Page 110: A Plague of Pigeons No. 1 (A1): Two high-flying pigeons have skedaddled. No. 2 (A2): The sparrow hawk might have had something to do with their flight. No. 3 (A5): One more bird has flown. No. 4 (B1): Polly wanna pigeon? No. 5 (B1 to B2): Another winged rat bites the dust. No. 6 (B3): His hair has been given a whole new part. No. 7 (B4 to B5): Two windows have been added to the balcony on the right. No. 8 (C2): It's now a hover pole. Nos. 9 and 10 (C3): His scarf is a tad longer, and his jacket has gained a button. No. 11 (D2 to E2): One of the missing birds might have resurfaced. No. 12 (D5): His sweat jacket is turning into a dress. No. 13 (E3): Yet another pigeon has landed. No. 14 (E3 to E4): His sneakers have become blue.

Page 112: Great Walls of China! Nos. 1 and 2 (A4): The tower is migrating, and the decoration on the far left of the banner has been upturned. No. 3 (A4 to B4): The door to the left has been bricked up. Nos. 4 and 5 (B2): Two loopholes have been bored into the top cornerstone, and the archway on the right has become level with its pal. No. 6 (B2 to C2): He's strolling down the wall, touching all the bricks. Nos. 7 and 8 (B3): A window is missing, so a red flag has been raised. No. 9 (C2): He's wearing a mood parka. No. 10 (C3 to D3): The mad genius in the furry hat and red scarf has grown four more heads and placed them on the bodies of her unsuspecting comrades. No. 11 (C5): Who ran off with the blue flag? No. 12 (D2): At least the sun is shining on his jacket. No. 13 (D3): A loophole has been removed. Nos. 14 and 15 (E2): The roving photographer is pointing her camera in the wrong direction; she needs to get a snap of the lady in the Santa cap. Nos. 16 and 17 (E3): When the woman in the brown jacket suddenly lost her feet, the guy holding the bag just had to take a step back.

Page 114: On the Waterfront No. 1 (A3 to B3): One string of lanterns has set itself apart. No. 2 (A4): The lonely conifer decided to make like a tree and leave. No. 3 (A4 to A5): The house down the way has had a roof-raising experience. Nos. 4 and 5 (A5): So its owners installed a window and strung up more lanterns. No. 6 (B4): The white shack has twice the shutters. No. 7 (C1 to D2): She took a dive. No. 8 (C2 to C3): That stairway has gone to heaven. No. 9 (C3): Her pole has floated off. Nos. 10 and 11 (C4 to D5): Not only is his boat chugging upstream, it also seems a little more festive. No. 12 (D1 to E3): The pilotless craft is starboard bound. No. 13 (D3 to D5): The vessel in the middle is casting a longer shadow. Nos. 14 and 15 (E2): It's become a nonsmoking boat with a spare tire.

Page 116: Slanted View No. 1 (A3): The crane is angling for a better position. No. 2 (B1): The top floor of that building now has a panoramic window. Nos. 3 and 4 (B2): The lamp and trees have grown. No. 5 (B2 to B3): And so has the tower. No. 6 (B3): The top of the signpost has been lopped off. No. 7 (B4): The balcony has been widened. Nos. 8 and 9 (C2): Someone's come to help unpack the car, and the female backpacker is slowly losing her shirt. No. 10 (C3): The house at the end of the block has become windowless. No. 11 (C4): It's a wonder his bag hasn't fallen off his back. No. 12 (D3): Her right shirtsleeve is inching toward her elbow. No. 13 (E1 to E2): The sidewalk has been narrowed by a hair. Nos. 14 and 15 (E4 to E5): His shorts and socks are surging toward each other.

Page 118: Where's My Prince? Nos. 1 and 2 (A1): He heard the ladies love a man with longer sleeves and ringless fingers. No. 3 (A2): He's put his hand out. No. 4 (A4): And his mirror image has emerged. No. 5 (B4): The blonde has put on her lucky stud. Nos. 6 and 7 (C3): Between the wart removal and the tongue cleaning, that creature is in the pink. No. 8 (C4 to C5): That extra pocket should come in handy. No. 9 (C5 to D5): Those stairs now get you nowhere. No. 10 (D2): Give him a kiss to build a toe on. No. 11 (E1): The rip in his jeans is getting bigger. No. 12 (E3): The beast's waterspout has lost its aim.

Page 119: **Not From Around Here** No. 1 (A5 to B5): Big Ben's getting taller. No. 2 (B3): One of the towers has gone AWOL. No. 3 (B4 to B5): Ol' Ben is losing track of time. No. 4 (C1): The captain has turned his boat around. No. 5 (C4): He's removed his T-shirt. Nos. 6 and 7 (C5): A lamp has vanished, and the bus has been given a new coat of paint. No. 8 (D1 to E1): The edge of the lower wall has come to the fore. No. 9 (D3): The arm of his sweater has been way outstretched. Nos. 10 and 11 (D4): The map has been enlarged for their viewing pleasure, and the teal trim on her tote is overtaking the checks. No. 12 (D5 to E5): The mortar line has moved to the right. No. 13 (E3): The stone has been split in two. No. 14 (E4): He's taken aback by their helpfulness, or at least his foot is.

Page 120: **A Leap of Faith** No. 1 (B2 to C1): A second ring of floats has surfaced. Nos. 2 and 3 (B2): Another skiff has dropped anchor, while the guy on the sailboat has wandered starboard. No. 4 (B2 to D4): The girls have changed their lineup. No. 5 (B3): And the pile in front of them has sunk. No. 6 (B3 to D3): The middle girl has become an Amazon. No. 7 (B3 to B4): The swim raft is drifting toward the other shore. No. 8 (B4): That clipper has gone cruising. No. 9 (B5): The distant dock has nearly doubled. No. 10 (C1 to D1): The pile on the left has mushroomed. No. 11 (C3): She's wearing the latest swimwear trend—the V-back. No. 12 (C4): The flower has turned to the other cheek. No. 13 (C5): The pile on the right has been capped. No. 14 (D1 to E5): The dock is receding. No. 15 (D4): The edge of the dock has been repaired. No. 16 (E3): A trio of planks has formed a union. No. 17 (E5): Now two boats can tie up here.

Page 122: **Rush Hour** No. 1 (A2): The flag decal has waned. No. 2 (A3 to B4): Lanky lads and lasses will have an easier time boarding the bus. No. 3 (B2): The gentleman has pulled his fingers inside the bus. No. 4 (B2 to B3): Those ladies have swapped seats. No. 5 (B5): His wristband has fallen off. No. 6 (C3): A portion of the cart's center pole has been hacked away. No. 7 (C4): The sleeve of his T-shirt has inched down. Nos. 8 and 9 (C5): The bus's serial number is minus a digit, and its wheel well has been covered with sheet metal. No. 10 (D1 to E2): The front wheel has been bent out of shape. No. 11 (D3): That electric rickshaw isn't going to get far without its battery cables. No. 12 (E4): The back hub has lost two lug nuts. No. 13 (E5): The fender has been curtailed.

Page 124: **Quite a Yarn** No. 1 (A1 to B1): The drainpipe has hopped to the right. No. 2 (A5): The blue tangle of yarn is hanging lower. Nos. 3 and 4 (B2 to B3): The warbler may have found a perch that'll keep it safe from cats, but the ever-growing hook might pose a new danger. No. 5 (B3): The cup has moved closer to the middle. No. 6 (B4): Another hook has been installed. No. 7 (B5 to C5): The pink skein of yarn is now a lovely shade of periwinkle. No. 8 (B5 to E5): The door has been widened. No. 9 (C1 to D1): The scarves are moving on up. Nos. 10 and 11 (C3): The small rug has been centered, and X has gotten a square. Nos. 12 and 13 (D4 to E4): The lantern is trying to hide behind the shortened pole. Nos. 14, 15, and 16 (E1): SUGAR has been inflated, the bucket has got a case of the blues, and the cat is cowering in the opposite direction.

Page 126: **Signs of Madness** No. 1 (A1): The circle is down a bulb. No. 2 (A1 to B1): Who stays at a wotel? Elmer Fudd? No. 3 (A4): Those Chinese characters are so heavy, they're sinking. No. 4 (B2): An *E* has flipped. No. 5 (B3): ON has become ONE, and THE, HE. No. 6 (B3 to C3): The arrow has lost its support. No. 7 (B4): The *P* and the *T* have exchanged locations. No. 8 (B5): Welcome to the Double *E*. No. 9 (C2 to D2): Wonder what's bewildered that beast? No. 10 (C2 to C3): The arrow's tail has been squared off. No. 11 (C4): If you like a little poetry and song with your moo shu, check out that joint. No. 12 (C4 to D4): That sign can be read only in rearview mirrors. No. 13 (C5): CABLE is now ABLE. No. 14 (D3 to E3): The bar signs have been here for so long, they no longer need a post to keep them up. No. 15 (E1): The *V* has turned into an *S*. No. 16 (E1 to E2): The 301 bus route has been downgraded to 300. No. 17 (E5): The parking restriction has been lifted.

Page 127: **Slip Into Something Comfortable** No. 1 (A1): The daisy has been spun. No. 2 (A3): Please, sir, may we have one more pink stripe? No. 3 (A5): That shoe has become just like his neighbor to the south. No. 4 (B2 to C3): Those two pairs have mixed it up. No. 5 (B3): The star of that shoe has gone on a holiday. No. 6 (B5): The deep blue shoe on the left has lost its middle dot. No. 7 (C4): The pink shoes seem to have fallen in love. No. 8 (C5): Two flowers have bloomed on the light green slipper. No. 9 (D2 to E2): Only a big set of toes could fill that shoe. No. 10 (D4): That red number was worn in *Torn Slipper*, one of Alfred Hitchcock's lesser-known gems. No. 11 (D5): The red and navy dots on the pale blue shoes are now sitting diagonally from one another. No. 12 (E1): The star's center has solidified. No. 13 (E5): That slipper is camera-shy.

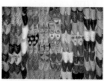

Page 128: **Enchanted Cottage** Nos. 1 and 2 (A2): The maple has lost a limb, but the bluebird's found a brand-new branch. No. 3 (A3): The window is just a bit fancier. No. 4 (A4): These shingles have satisfied their urge to merge. No. 5 (A5): The railing has crashed into the tree. No. 6 (B2): That pillar is so busted. No. 7 (B2 to C2): The sign has been embiggened. No. 8 (B3 to C3): That's Captain Corner to you. No. 9 (B4): Another flowerpot has been strung up. Nos. 10, 11, and 12 (B5): A 5 has been added to the address, the bird has alighted from the balcony to the gutter, and the top section of the drainpipe has been stretched. Nos. 13 and 14 (C1): The birdbath is making a slow getaway and has gained a fine feathered friend in the process. No. 15 (D1 to D2): The maple has moved closer to home. No. 16 (E3): It's a plainer post now. No. 17 (E3 to E4): The sunbeam is creeping up the lawn.

[GENIUS]

Page 132: **Bite of the Apple** No. 1 (A2): The left side of her hat has been bleached. No. 2 (A3): The top level of the building's gradation has been pushed forward. Nos. 3 and 4 (A5): As the skyscraper goes up, so do the horse's ears. No. 5 (B2): She's gone from a grin to a smirk. No. 6 (B5): A stud has popped off the blinder. No. 7 (C1): The strap is short a loop. Nos. 8 and 9 (C2): Both these purses have stitching issues. Nos. 10 and 11 (C3): The shaft has been extended, and a rivet has

departed. No. 12 (C5): The turn signal atop the cab has disappeared. No. 13 (D1): An extra fastener has been added to her jeans. No. 14 (D4): That taxi has lost a wheel. No. 15 (D5): The lead has crossed paths with the rein. No. 16 (E1): The drain has been widened. No. 17 (E2): Her pants are longer.

Page 134: **Man Overboard** No. 1 (A2): The girl with a pearl earring is haunting that apartment. No. 2 (A3): The chimney has been transplanted. Nos. 3 and 4 (A4): The top floor now gets more light, and a masked madam is taking in the scenery. No. 5 (A5 to B5): A flag has been run up the pole. No. 6 (C1 to D1): One window has widened its view. No. 7 (C2 to D2): And another has become just like the one above it. No. 8 (C3): The blinds have been lowered. No. 9 (C4): The mooring post has vaulted up. No. 10 (D1): That's one damaged pillar. Nos. 11 and 12 (D2): The gondolier and the kayaker have shipped off. Nos. 13 and 14 (D3): A staircase has washed away, while the two men in the alley have traded places. No. 15 (D5): Did someone order a *grande ferro* for the front of the gondola? No. 16 (E2): The straw hat has been refashioned to suit a big wig.

Page 136: **Beachside Feast** No. 1 (A1): A balcony has inched its way into the picture. No. 2 (B5): Upon every sky, a little cloud must form. No. 3 (C2 to D2): A sunbather has joined the crowd. No. 4 (C3): A bloom has fallen off the umbrella. Nos. 5, 6, 7, and 8 (C4): The boys along the shore have swapped spots, the man near them has distanced himself from his pals, the lamp has spread its wings, and the hose has been disconnected. No. 9 (C4 to D4): The trash receptacle has flipped its lid as well as its can. Nos. 10 and 11 (C5): A parasol has blown away, while a new guy is soaking up some rays. No. 12 (D1 to D2): Her earring is stone-free. Nos. 13 and 14 (D2): The glass has ditched its shadow, and the corners of her sandwich are making finer points. Nos. 15 and 16 (D3): Three straws are better than two, and everything will come up roses for her in those sunglasses. No. 17 (D3 to D4): The lamppost's shadow has been erased. Nos. 18 and 19 (D4): The straw is riding higher, but the tray could use a support bar. Nos. 20 and 21 (D5): He can see clearly now; his Ray-Bans are gone. And it's high-tide time for the concrete slab. No. 22 (E3): The bottom of the umbrella pole has dropped out.

Page 138: **No Contest** No. 1 (A3 to B3): The camel has craned his neck. No. 2 (B2 to D2): The biker has been working out. No. 3 (B2 to B3): Three stories have been shaved off that building. No. 4 (B3 to B4): The jockey has given up his reins. No. 5 (B5): Plus, his riding crop has been cropped. No. 6 (C3 to D3): The crew chief has found a pair of shades to nibble on. No. 7 (C3): We've heard of sudden hair loss, but that guy's got it bad. No. 8 (C4 to C5): His saddle is strapless. Nos. 9 and 10 (D1): The road has vanished in the dust, and the fender is even redder. Nos. 11 and 12 (D2): The star decal is golden and has more to say. No. 13 (D3): The first 4 has flipped. No. 14 (D4): The stripes on Baldy's shorts have broken up. No. 15 (D5): The van is moving at a good clip. No. 16 (D5 to E5): The camel's right rear leg has taken a baby step back. No. 17 (E1): The wheel has shed many spokes. No. 18 (E2): The biker has lifted himself off the ground. No. 19 (E3): His shorts are hanging lower. No. 20 (E4 to E5): The plateau beneath them has been uplifted.

Page 140: **Castle in the Sand** No. 1 (A3): The tree branches are spreading out. No. 2 (A5 to B5): The tower on the far right has spun itself around. No. 3 (B2 to C2): The organ's pipes have been given a boost. No. 4 (B4): You can change its name, but it's still the same old fortress. No. 5 (C4): The top two rays of the nimbus have breached the arch. No. 6 (D2): That guy in the blue is new. Nos. 7 and 8 (D3): The castle trim is down a brick, and the boy in the jersey has lost his visor. No. 9 (D3 to E3): The girl in the red shirt has reversed her position. Nos. 10, 11, 12, and 13 (D4): The king of this castle has earned a star, cocked an eyebrow, and widened his pupils. Perhaps it has something to do with the woman's revamped hair hue. No. 14 (D5 to E5): A growth spurt like hers will definitely leave stretch marks. No. 15 (E1): The center stripe on his shirt is now solidly maroon. No. 16 (E2): The blue pennant has fluttered away. Nos. 17, 18, and 19 (E4): The brunette's hair and the redhead's jacket have been lengthened, and could someone give that lady a hand?

Page 142: **Tea and Sympathy** Nos. 1 and 2 (A1): The price board is heading inside, and 88 quid seems a bit dear for a five-course dinner here. No. 3 (A3 to B3): Who pinched the flower? No. 4 (A5): An *I* has said good-bye. No. 5 (B2): The plug has been pulled on that sign. No. 6 (B3): Instead of the shoreline, the patrons of this establishment can take in the sights of tunnels, trains, and automobiles. No. 7 (B4 to B5): The wood on the bottom window sash has become bloated. No. 8 (C1 to D1): The tiles behind our hostess have been grouted anew. No. 9 (D1 to E1): Her shirt is providing more coverage. No. 10 (D2): She can't seem to get a handle on the watering can. No. 11 (D3): That *A* is on its way to being a *V*. No. 12 (D4 to E4): The picket is making quite a point. Nos. 13 and 14 (D5): The ear of the wooden chair is stretching out, and the flowers have been rearranged. No. 15 (E2): Another eyelet bloom has sprouted on her apron. No. 16 (E3): The fence is minus a post. No. 17 (E5): The upholstery has been put on backward.

Page 143: **Hagglers' Haven** No. 1 (B1): The clothesline pole has reached a new level. Nos. 2 and 3 (C2): The flutist is suddenly myopic, and the minivan has turned that back wheel around. Nos. 4, 5, and 6 (C3): Off in the background, the blue cap has grown quite a brim. Maybe that's what caught the attention of the woman in the turquoise camisole. And the sarong on the dude in the white shirt has become much more demure. Nos. 7 and 8 (C4): She'd better pony up the cash for that necklace. Meanwhile, a guy in a white tee has appeared near the back stall. No. 9 (C4 to D4): The girl in the blue shorts is trying on a braided bracelet. Nos. 10, 11, and 12 (D3): The red and blue corks have been switched, and there's a new ring for sale. By the way, how do you play *dards*? Nos. 13 and 14 (E3): The walking stick has been decorated with more beads, and one of the wee turtles has fled the pink keepsake box. No. 15 (E4): The knife has turned. No. 16 (E5): That parking spot is no longer delineated.

Page 144: Whatever Floats Your Boat

No. 1 (A2): Perhaps that radar dome has been filled with helium. No. 2 (A3): The second diagonal of the *X* is venturing outside it boundaries. No. 3 (A4): Radio reception on that island has been improved. No. 4 (B4): The crew should count the lifeboats again. Nos. 5 and 6 (B5 to C5): The bow has been enlarged, and a few floors have been added to the seaside condos on the far right. No. 7 (C1): The bars have come off the windows of that building. Nos. 8, 9, and 10 (C2): Another skiff has appeared in the harbor, an extra cooler has been loaded onto the boat in front of it, and the cargo hauler behind them is slowly sinking. Nos. 11, 12, 13, and 14 (C3): A plethora of portholes has been added to the promenade deck, the boat below has completely dropped its anchor, the vessel to its right has stretched out, and the yacht has done a 180. Nos. 15, 16, and 17 (C5): That craft is drifting toward the ocean liner, the dock has been extended, and a passenger on the ferry has come up for some sun. No. 18 (D1): The DRAGON has been centered. No. 19 (D2 to E2): The white umbrella is midway through its transformation into a tent. No. 20 (D3): That boy has been pulled back by the tide. No. 21 (D4): A swimmer is exploring deeper waters. No. 22 (D4 to D5): The blue umbrella panel must have forgotten to lather on the sunscreen. Nos. 23, 24, and 25 (D5): The Angels cap is long in the bill, the undertow has taken the dark-haired girl a long way from where she started, and the 7 has been changed to a 6. No. 26 (D5 to E5): Father and son are now splashing around on the left. No. 27 (E1): A beach chair has been freed up. No. 28 (E2): The guy in the black trunks has shifted to the right.

[LIFE CLASSICS]

Page 148: Anchors Aweigh

No. 1 (B2): His football has entered another dimension. No. 2 (B3): An extra row of rivets has been added to the funnel on the left. No. 3 (B4 to B5): And what happened to the other flue? No. 4 (C1 to E1): The boy is launching himself toward the wormhole that stole his ball. No. 5 (C3): The lamp has been raised a tad. No. 6 (C4): Her handle is getting a little out of hand. No. 7 (D3): That toddler is easily distracted. No. 8 (D3 to E3): And he's fidgeting his left foot.

Page 150: Motel California

No. 1 (A3 to A4): The palm on the right has sprouted a few fronds to match its neighbor. No. 2 (C1): A 4 has been added to confuse the mailman. Nos. 3 and 4 (C3): The *E* has turned backward, while the address above the second arch has scooted to the left. Nos. 5 and 6 (C5): The chimney has been pushed aside, and a window has vanished. Nos. 7 and 8 (D2): There's no VACANCY sign now, and the entryway above the car has been given a roof extension. No. 9 (D3): A girl has come out to play. No. 10 (D4): The window's panes have been halved. No. 11 (D5): The convertible's fender is suffering from chrome deficiency. No. 12 (E1): A planter has been set out. No. 13 (E2 to E5): The street has gained an extra lane. No. 14 (E4): The hubcap has gone concave.

Page 151: Who's Minding the Shore?

No. 1 (B2 to C2): The lifesaver has been given a more central position. No. 2 (B3 to C3): He can't stop pacing. No. 3 (B5): That tree is headed for a more distant shore. No. 4 (C1): An extra bench has appeared. No. 5 (C2): The back of the stairwell has dropped its shadow. No. 6 (C3): The umbrella has hopped over the lounger. No. 7 (C3 to C4): Another chair has been added. No. 8 (C5 to D5): The boat is tetherless. No. 9 (D1 to E1): And it's been shortened.

Page 152: Summer Shuffle

No. 1 (A2): The flagpole has lost its top. No. 2 (A3): The shelter has been granted a longer eave. No. 3 (A5): Trees grow fast in this part of town. No. 4 (B1): That cheater has a telescoping handle. No. 5 (B2): And now he knows what time it is. No. 6 (B4): The row of backstops has been halved. No. 7 (C1 to E3): Is it legal to widen the court mid-game? No. 8 (C2): Another puck has shown up. No. 9 (C3): He can play one-footed. No. 10 (D2): An *F* has shuffled off. No. 11 (D4): And the 7 has joined it. No. 12 (E5): The puck has been flung off court.

Page 154: Up the Creek

No. 1 (A4 to B4): The smokestack is taller. No. 2 (B3): AND has been changed to OR. No. 3 (C2): The roof of the refreshment stand is showing some real growth potential. No. 4 (C4): The window is no longer divided. No. 5 (C5 to D5): The life preserver has shifted left. No. 6 (D2): The back paddler has been capped. No. 7 (D3): Another canoeist has floated in. No. 8 (D4): The space between the top two spokes has been filled. No. 9 (D5 to E5): The canoe has become roomier. No. 10 (E2): A school of piranhas has dined on her fingers. No. 11 (E4): And the bottom of his oar, too.

Page 156: The Complete Camper

No. 1 (A4): The fish have been switched. No. 2 (B1 to B2): Will a shorter rod catch smaller fish? No. 3 (B2): Like that one? No. 4 (B3): The raft has been pumped up. No. 5 (B3 to C4): The water bag is slightly bigger. No. 6 (B4 to C4): The grill is gone. No. 7 (B4 to D4): Someone's pulled the curtain on this campy scene. No. 8 (C1): More headroom has been tacked on the air mattress. No. 9 (C2 to C3): The foot of the boot has been stretched. No. 10 (C3): The oar has gotten longer. Nos. 11 and 12 (C5): Both the car door and the stockpot have lost their handles. No. 13 (D1 to E1): The campers have decided to take a java-free journey. No. 14 (D3): The cooler will be harder to haul. No. 15 (D5): A bar on that bench has been crossed with another. No. 16 (D5 to E5): The stove is moving closer to the table. No. 17 (E1): The radio has been given an extra dial. No. 18 (E3): A rung has been added to the rack. No. 19 (E5): The stove is down a knob.

Page 158: Folding Their Tent

No. 1 (B2 to D2): Camping has totally turned her around. No. 2 (B5): A crate has been removed from the roof rack. Nos. 3 and 4 (C1): The boy has taken his left elbow out of hiding, and a gaggle of paddlers is rowing toward the clan. No. 5 (C3): Someone has clambered onto the dock. No. 6 (C4): The window has been revamped. No. 7 (D1 to E1): He's kicked the cooler to the curb. No. 8 (D4): His sock is slipping down. No. 9 (D4 to D5): The taillight's center has receded. No. 10 (E3): One of the poles has been pulled back.

Page 160: **Occidental Oasis** No. 1 (A1): The stack has been given a little heft. No. 2 (B4): A scalloped center has brightened that dark umbrella. Nos. 3 and 4 (B5): An additional spotlight and waiter have been installed. No. 5 (C1 to D1): Her seat doubles as a flotation device. No. 6 (C5): The poolside ledge has been widened. No. 7 (D1 to D2): A third rail has been added. No. 8 (D3): The diving board is reaching beyond the deep end. No. 9 (D5): He's spun the top of the bass to the left. No. 10 (E2): The bottom step on the right has shed its nosing. No. 11 (E2 to E3): He wants next dibs on the diving board. No. 12 (E3): SPRINGS has become singular. Nos. 13 and 14 (E4): The riser beneath the last step has been broadened, and a line has been drawn down those tiles.

Page 162: **Suiteless in Seattle** No. 1 (A2): The power lines have been rewired. No. 2 (B2 to B3): If you were expecting DELUXE accommodations, brace yourself for the agony of DE TOE. No. 3 (B3): Guess someone has to phone MR. VOOM. No. 4 (C1 to D1): Well, at least that room offers a wider view. Nos. 5 and 6 (C3): That car lot no longer sells used cars. And *Y* has that sign been changed? Nos. 7 and 8 (C4): The streetlamp is branching out, and that joint really puts the *ZZZ*'s in PIZZA. No. 9 (C5): The *E* is lacking its neon luster. No. 10 (D2 to D3): A motel after our own hearts. No. 11 (D3): Pity the passenger who needs to get in that car door. Nos. 12, 13, and 14 (D4): The arrow and the *M* are pointing in the wrong direction, and the truck is having wheel trouble. No. 15 (D5): A car has turned off the road. No. 16 (E1 to E2): The ramp has been removed. No. 17 (E5): The flagpole has jumped over the hedge.